Scripture quotations marked (NIV) are taken from the Holy Bible, New International Version®, NIV®. Copyright © 1973, 1978, 1984, 2011 by Biblica, Inc.™ Used by permission of Zondervan. All rights reserved worldwide. www.zondervan.com The "NIV" and "New International Version" are trademarks registered in the United States Patent and Trademark Office by Biblica, Inc.™

Lies, all Lies

By

Gerry Fox

Lies, all Lies

By

Gerry Fox

Copyright © 2018 by Gerry Fox

All rights reserved.

This book or any portion thereof may not be reproduced or used in any manner whatsoever without the express written permission of the publisher except for the use of brief quotations in a book review.

Printed in Canada

First printing, 2019

ISBN 978-1-7752079-2-4

Table of Contents

Introduction..1
Chapter One - Where All Prophecy Begins............................3
Chapter Two - The Treasonous Affair......................................8
Chapter Three - The Great Heresy?..31
Chapter Four - A Final Proof, The River of Living Water.....55
Conclusion - The Errors of Our Ways....................................58
Epilogue..66

"Treason is a matter of the date, Proctor"
— *Pierce Brown, Morning Star*

Introduction

"The word of the Lord came to me: "Son of man, set your face against Gog, of the land of Magog, the chief prince of Meshek and Tubal; prophesy against him and say: 'This is what the Sovereign Lord says: I am against you, Gog, chief prince of Meshek and Tubal. I will turn you around, put hooks in your jaws and bring you out with your whole army—your horses, your horsemen fully armed, and a great horde with large and small shields, all of them brandishing their swords. Persia, Cush and Put will be with them, all with shields and helmets, also Gomer with all its troops, and Beth Togarmah from the far north with all its troops—the many nations with you." (Ezekiel 38:1–6)

Since about the time of World War I, a prophecy has circulated among the Church, claiming that Russia and Germany, along with a number of other countries like Ethiopia, are the nations of Gog and Magog referenced in the book of Ezekiel chapter 38 and 39. This prophecy is also used as the basis for the rebirth of the nation of Israel, for indeed, how could it ever be fulfilled if an Israel of God didn't exist in the Promised Land?

Given the rise of communism and fascism in these nations and the violence of the past two world wars, this interpretation seemed plausible. Considering the political changes since then, however, can we still apply that interpretation today? Does the current Israel truly have something to concern itself with? I would argue no. Do not be deceived, Jesus said (Luke 21:8). I believe a great error, and perhaps even a deception, has occurred. In this book, we will look at deciphering the who, what, why, and where of it all.

Chapter One - Where All Prophecy Begins

> "Do not weep! See, the Lion of the tribe of Judah, the Root of David, has triumphed. He is able to open the scroll and its seven seals... You are worthy to take the scroll and to open its seals, because you were slain, and with your blood you purchased for God persons from every tribe and language and people and nation."
> (Revelation 5:5, 9)

If we hope to make sense of any of the prophecies of the Bible, we must begin with the end of the story—the last chapters of the book of Revelation—and work backward to the beginning. With Jesus Christ's death and resurrection, we were given the end of all matters where prophecy is concerned, so no prophecy or book takes precedent over what we find in the Revelation of Christ Jesus.

This is especially the case where Gog and Magog are concerned, because what we find mentioned in Ezekiel 38–39 is restated in Revelation 20, but with an addition. Now, why would that be? Is there something significant to it? Are these the same groups of nations mentioned in Ezekiel? More foundational, though, is this: why does God refer to these nations and people as Gog and Magog in the first place?

Scripture reveals to us that Gog and Magog are names of people, first and foremost. Magog was the name of one of Noah's grandsons near the beginning of recorded time (Genesis 10:2) and Gog is the name of one of Reuben's grandsons, circa 4004 B.C. (1 Chronicles 5:4). Beyond this, we aren't told much else except that, where Noah's sons and grandsons are concerned, the nations were established *"according to their lines of descent"* (Genesis 10:32). As for Gog and the Reubenites, not only were they of the tribe of Israel but they were a military-trained bunch (1 Chronicles 5:19, 24). It's very interesting, if not highly significant, that a connection to the nation of Israel exists here, and twice no less. First, the Reubenites' father was the firstborn of Israel who lost his birthright to Joseph for defiling his father's bed. A very grievous and serious sin! We are then told that the Reubenites ended up as traitors of God because they decided to follow idols. They betrayed God even after He helped them in their war against the Hagrites (1 Chronicles 5:25). Note the words:

> "But they were unfaithful to the God of their ancestors and prostituted themselves to the gods of the peoples of the land, whom God had destroyed before them. So the God of Israel stirred up the spirit of Pul king of Assyria (that is, Tiglath-Pileser king of Assyria), who took the Reubenites, the Gadites and the half-tribe of Manasseh into exile." (1 Chronicles 5:25–26)

This is quite interesting, because it tells us that they were traitors. Treason, as we shall see shortly, is why Gog and Magog will be destroyed. The important thing to understand here is that God uses figurative language and historical types to explain and describe events. This is one of the keys to unlocking prophecy. We must understand how typology works, and the best illustration is surely where the book of Revelation refers to Jerusalem as "Sodom and Egypt":

> ...which is figuratively called Sodom and Egypt—where also their Lord was crucified. (Revelation 11:8)

Here we have both the figurative and literal in play, and why does God do this? Well, ultimately it has everything to do with faithlessness and idolatry. Both Egypt and Sodom knew who God was, saw His work, and yet were blatantly faithless and rebellious. Jerusalem was likewise faithless and rebellious, and still is in our current day and age. Note that halfway through the great tribulation, with Armageddon staring them in the face, the people of Jerusalem will still deal with idolatry. It's referred to as the Abomination of Desolation.

The prophecy of Zechariah recognizes this as well (Zechariah 12:10–13:6). Imagine if it were against the law to speak about Christ Jesus in Jerusalem, with the Lord banned from His own city and even cursed! How utterly unbelievable would this be, especially in view of how everything is written beforehand? It's not for nothing that we read about the crying and wailing that will accompany Christ Jesus to His city (Zechariah 12:10). Imagine, if you will, one having spent a good portion of one's life rejecting and even cursing the true Messiah only to turn around and see Him with your own eyes! The pain of this will be excruciating, the people's remorse so severe that, as Zechariah teaches, the Lord God will declare,

> *"On that day, I will banish the names of the idols from the land, and they will be remembered no more," declares the Lord Almighty. "I will remove both the prophets and the spirit of impurity from the land. And if anyone still prophesies, their father and mother, to whom they were born, will say to them, 'You must die, because you have told lies in the Lord's name.' Then their own parents will stab the one who prophesies."*
> (Zechariah 13:2–3)

Idolatry will be wiped out for good. In the meantime, all we currently have are lies, lies, and more lies, and this from the city of Jerusalem and in the name of God! Shocking, isn't it? So, the analogy Sodom and Egypt fits.

Make note, though, that of all the prophecies in the Bible, we have no need for special revelation of any kind here. God simply makes the words understandable to anyone who cares to read them. Indeed, not even a child could get this prophecy wrong.

Now, as for Magog, nothing else is mentioned about him personally in scripture, but it can be inferred that he turned out to be a turncoat as well. It's interesting that Magog was mentioned at the beginning of recorded time (Genesis 10:2) and again at the end of recorded time (Revelation 20:8).

So why does God use these names, Gog and Magog? Simple! He sees in these future people the same kind of behavior as these previous generations did, but with the twist of having to punish and destroy them with a deluge of fire and brimstone from out of heaven. In the past, God used foreign kings to exact judgment, but now God will judge and punish these people from out of heaven. But why?

This brings us to our next question. Are these the same groups of nations mentioned in Ezekiel? Given the similarities, it sure looks that way. Consider these verses:

> "But fire came down from heaven and devoured them." (Revelation 20:9)

> "I will pour down torrents of rain, hailstones and burning sulfur…" (Ezekiel 38:22)

> "In number they are like the sand on the seashore." (Revelation 20:8)

> "You will advance against my people Israel like a cloud that covers the land." (Ezekiel 38:16)

> *"Persia, Cush and Put will be with them... Gomer with all its troops, and Beth Togarmah from the far north with all its troops—the many nations with you."* (Ezekiel 38:5-6)

> *"...and will go out to deceive the nations in the four corners of the earth—Gog and Magog—and to gather them for battle."* (Revelation 20:8)

Are these not practically identical, with just a few minor differences? Note that the scriptures refer to these nations as coming not just out of the north (from Israel's perspective) but from every corner of the world. This can't be overlooked.

The two prophecies are the same. There can be no argument about this. Why, though, are these people going to be judged and destroyed in such harsh ways? The current interpretation would have us believe that it's because they are going to attack Israel. This is not what the Bible teaches, however, as we shall see in our next chapter.

Chapter Two - The Treasonous Affair

"I the Lord search the heart and examine the mind, to reward each person according to their conduct, according to what their deeds deserve." (Jeremiah 17:10)

Treason is a despicable crime. It dishonours the individual and betrays one's own country to foreign powers—worse, a traitor betrays one's own family. Where God is concerned, treason is without question the worst of all crimes, period, because one is literally betraying the One who created us in the first place. It is the one behaviour God hates above all, and it is punished severely by Him.

"A nation can survive its fools, and even the ambitious. But it cannot survive treason from within. An enemy at the gates is less formidable, for he is known and carries his banner openly. But the traitor moves amongst those within the gate freely, his sly whispers rustling through all the alleys, heard in the very halls of government itself. For the traitor appears not a traitor; he speaks in accents familiar to his victims, and he wears their face and their arguments, he appeals to the baseness that lies deep in the hearts of all men. He rots the soul of a nation, he works secretly and unknown in the night to undermine the pillars of the city, he infects the body politic so that it can no longer resist. A murderer is less to fear."
— *Marcus Tullius Cicero*

We see this quite clearly in the Old Testament, especially in the life of Israel and the Reubenites and their grandson Gog in the battle against the Hagrites. They betrayed God even after He helped them win that war. Therefore, God needs to test and examine our faith and character: because His glory and reputation requires it. Job and Isaiah provide prime examples of this:

> *"But he knows the way that I take; when he has tested me, I will come forth as gold." (Job 23:10)*
>
> *"See, I have refined you, though not as silver; I have tested you in the furnace of affliction. For my own sake, for my own sake, I do this. How can I let myself be defamed? I will not yield my glory to another." (Isaiah 48:10–11)*

A people chosen by God must be faithful to Him period. It is an imperative, otherwise God ends up being defamed, and He takes that extremely seriously; as a righteous and holy individual, He cannot allow Himself to be a party to sin. His relationship with us is therefore a difficult one, because when we prove unfaithful it reflects upon Him—if, that is, He were to bless us in some way. It is an issue that continues even into the New Testament and to our own lives today. Never make the mistake of thinking that God is finished with anyone of us!

> *"In all this you greatly rejoice, though now for a little while you may have had to suffer grief in all kinds of trials. These have come so that the proven genuineness of your faith—of greater worth than gold, which perishes even though refined by fire—may result in praise, glory and honor when Jesus Christ is revealed." {1 Peter 1:5-7}*

So, perfection is what God is after in our lives and it is why Satan is called the accuser of the brethren. He tries to come between us and God constantly. Nothing gives Satan greater pleasure than proving God wrong. It empowers him like nothing else.

Side Note

Of all the doctrines in the Bible that should be taught and understood thoroughly, demonology, Satanism, and spiritual warfare should be studied particularly. Unfortunately, this is not the case. In fact, many churches, if not every society on planet earth want nothing to do with these teachings, or they take them to be fables and fairy tales. That is a grave mistake. Satan is a very real creature. One need only study the events regarding the Mothman of Virginia to see a perfect example of a fallen angel who plays god with people's lives. Either read the book or watch the movie.

Everything about those events and this creature is well spelled out and explained in Job 33:15-24. This Mothman is Satan. How frightening it is that governments are aware of supernatural forces. Instead of taking the Bible at its word, they choose to think and believe otherwise:

"The U.S. Government is being taken over by the space people!"

This rumour spread throughout the country in 1967, an updated version of the old devil theory. Actually, it got its start in 1949 when James V. Forrestal, the brilliant secretary of defence in the Truman cabinet, went bananas and raced through the corridors of the Pentagon screaming, "We're being invaded and we can't stop them!" He was convinced that his phones were being tapped and some enormous conspiracy was underway. Soon after he was placed in a hospital, he leaped out a window to his death. While the press blamed his paranoia on the tensions of the cold war, the UFO enthusiasts knew better. Air force Intelligence had compiled a Top-Secret Estimate of the Situation following their UFO investigations in 1947-48. Their conclusion, according to the late Capt. Edward Ruppelt, was that flying saucers were extra-terrestrial. Forrestal, so the story went, was one of the few to read that report before Air Force Chief of Staff Hoyt Vandenburg ordered all copies destroyed and it blew his mind.

Two other top military men, Gen. George C. Marshall and Gen. Douglas MacArthur were obsessed with the flying saucer phenomenon. MacArthur made several public statements declaring the next war would be fought against "evil beings from outer space." A fabled "think tank," the Rand Corporation, was assigned to feed UFO data into a computer and fight an imaginary war with those evil beings. Since we wouldn't know where they are from, what their technology was, or how to attack their bases, the computer advised us to surrender."[1]

Isn't this something? Governments and their agencies (like the military and CIA) probably have dossiers full of strange and inexplicable happenings. What they call 'space people' the bible calls fallen angels and demons! I myself had an encounter with such 'space people' if one desires to call them that. It was a matter of God Himself teaching me the reality of it. It occurred when I was just 18 years old and a new convert to Christ. That day started out uneventful enough with me working an early morning shift at a local restaurant and finished about noon. I arrived home to an empty house and upon entering and making my way up the stairs to my bedroom I turned the corner and was about to enter the bedroom when I was pushed into the wall on the left-hand side of the hallway opposite the closet. Someone literally shoved me into the wall! This shook me up of course, and I immediately went into prayer and was in a state of prayer for quite some time pleading for God to help me. I asked for His protection and after what seemed like an hour or, so I felt strong enough to go about my regular day and nothing else out of the ordinary happened. When the next day arrived, however, and after having worked another morning shift, I again arrived home to an empty house. Upon entering and again making my way up the stairs to my bedroom to change and shower, I again was pushed into the wall on the left-hand side opposite the closet. This time, however, I literally

---

[1] John A. Keel, *The Mothman Prophecies* (New York, NY: Tom Doherty Associates LLC, 1975), 21 –217.

felt a hand doing the pushing. I felt it hand on my bicep as it pushed me right into the door jam. My baby toe was bruised black and blue from the way I landed into the door jam. This immediately sent me into prayer again and this time it wasn't for a mere hour but several hours of intense prayer for help and protection. I also put on some music and worshipped God knowing that such an environment of praise was detrimental to Satan's presence and was in this state of worship and prayer. It was then that I experienced a wonderful feeling of peace that washed over me. It was an incredible all-consuming peace that went through my entire being from head to toe and I knelt there just bathed in this peace and was filled with love like I had never known it. I got through to God and He got through to me and for the rest of the evening I read and studied the bible while turning my thoughts to Sunday and what a fascinating testimony this was going to make. Little did I know though what God had in store.

When Sunday arrived, I was a most miserable person having slept in which meant I was going to miss Church which upset me terribly. I quickly got ready and practically ran the entire way to Church and arrived when the worship part of the service was just coming to an end. The church was full that morning and for me, the only empty seat was in the back-row corner aisle which was a little upsetting since I enjoyed sitting closer to the action near the front. In any case I sat down and was quite agitated with excitement about the previous day's events. An excitement which turned even more astonishing because that morning we had a guest preacher by the name of Dr. Jefferies. He was a professor of theology from a bible college from California and lo and behold he was speaking about spiritual warfare taking his text from Ephesians 6:10-18 the full text of which reads:

> *"Finally, be strong in the Lord and in his mighty power. Put on the full armour of God, so that you can take your stand against the devil's schemes. For our struggle is not against flesh and blood, but against the*

rulers, against the authorities, against the powers of this dark world and against the spiritual forces of evil in the heavenly realms. Therefore, put on the full armour of God, so that when the day of evil comes, you may be able to stand your ground, and after you have done everything, to stand. Stand firm then, with the belt of truth buckled around your waist, with the breastplate of righteousness in place, and with your feet fitted with the readiness that comes from the gospel of peace. In addition to all this, take up the shield of faith, with which you can extinguish all the flaming arrows of the evil one. Take the helmet of salvation and the sword of the Spirit, which is the word of God.
And pray in the Spirit on all occasions with all kinds of prayers and requests. With this in mind, be alert and always keep on praying for all the Lord's people."

Now to say that I was stunned, flabbergasted to be hearing this of all things is of course an understatement. I sat there wide eyed and fixated on every word and could hardly contain myself wanting to jump up and testify to the truth of what this man was preaching and was about to do just that when suddenly, a hand touched me on the top of my right shoulder. I was sitting there in the back row wearing a black leather coat when suddenly, a hand touched me on my right shoulder. It was a strange kind of feeling because unlike a normal hand this one penetrated the flesh. There was no pressure upon the jacket but rather this hand went right through the leather jacket, shirt and into the flesh of the shoulder. This hand then compressed its hand upon my shoulder as if to comfort me. I immediately turned my head around to see who was doing this only to be faced with the back wall. Wow, I almost jumped out of my seat but seeing how I was going to disrupt the service and wanting to hear everything this man was saying and teaching I remained seated and felt as though God was telling me to be at peace and pay attention to what this minister had to say because it is important which I did of course. After church there was no way of trying to speak with our guest and decided that the evening service would be the better venue as it is not so formal. I left the church that morning with a new-found respect for the teachings of the bible regarding spiritual warfare and how we are very much in a war with spiritual powers. The realm of the supernatural became very real to me as it should to everyone. For a future Gog and Magog, this is especially pertinent.

*   *   *

So, in the end, God's glory and reputation requires that He test and purify us. In a coming future battle with Almighty God, Gog and Magog, who are the worst offenders of all, will learn the truth of this—painfully so. Their sin is treason, pure and simple, but a treason of a kind so serious in magnitude that it could only be comparable to the rebellion of the angels themselves during the beginning of the world. How do we know this? By simply looking at what is revealed the book of Revelation, where we find some very interesting additions to the original prophecy in Ezekiel. Consider this:

> *"When the thousand years are over,*
>
> *Satan will be released from his prison and will*
>
> *go out to deceive the nations in the four*

> *corners of the earth—Gog and Magog—and to gather them for battle. In number they are like the sand on the seashore. They marched across the breadth of the earth and surrounded the camp of God's people, the city he loves. But fire came down from heaven and devoured them. And the devil, who deceived them, was thrown into the lake of burning sulfur, where the beast and the false prophet had been thrown. They will be tormented day and night for ever and ever." (Revelation 20:7–10)*

And this:

> *"And I saw an angel coming down out of heaven, having the key to the Abyss and holding in his hand a great chain. He seized the dragon, that ancient serpent, who is the devil, or Satan, and bound him for a thousand years. He threw him into the Abyss, and locked and sealed it over him, to keep him from deceiving the nations anymore until the thousand years were ended. After that, he must be set free for a short time." (Revelation 20:1–3)*

Now, pay attention here. This teaches us that there is a coming period—a full millennium, in fact—whereby with the return of Christ Jesus to Jerusalem (the first resurrection, Revelation 20:4-6), due to Armageddon, the world is to undergo a transformation of sorts. Satan will be cast into the abyss, and this will cause all sin (or wilful sin) to stop dead cold upon the Earth. Why? Because the blindness that now affects mankind (2 Corinthians 4:4) by way of Satan's power, along with his deceiving/lying ways, will have been extinguished and vanquished.

> *"The god of this age has blinded the minds of unbelievers, so that they cannot see the light of the gospel that displays the glory of Christ, who is the image of God." (2 Corinthians 4:4)*

Obedience to God will occur as an almost automatic response due to people's eyes being opened to the truth. As a result, Earth will be transformed, and peace will reign throughout the world in the aftermath of Armageddon. Like Abraham of old visiting the ruins of Sodom and Gomorrah after their destruction, so too will Earth's survivors make their way among the ruined cities of the world, rebuilding what they can. With Christ's Kingship, mankind will come to experience and live in a world abundant in love, joy, peace, patience, kindness, goodness, faithfulness (Galatians 5:22), and all the other good things that righteousness bestows upon us in abundance.

Everything will change under the leadership of Christ, particularly faith, which will no longer be a struggle. People will experience plentiful faith day in and day out. Like the very angels in heaven, they will know who God is. The scriptures make this perfectly and abundantly clear:

"And I will pour out on the house of David and the inhabitants of Jerusalem a spirit of grace and supplication. They will look on me, the one they have pierced, and they will mourn for him as one mourns for an only child and grieve bitterly for him as one grieves for a firstborn son." (Zechariah 12:10)

"I saw thrones on which were seated those who had been given authority to judge. And I saw the souls of those who had been beheaded because of their testimony about Jesus and because of the word of God. They had not worshiped the beast or its image and had not received its mark on their foreheads or their hands. They came to life and reigned with Christ a thousand years. (The rest of the dead did not come to life until the thousand years were ended.) This is the first resurrection. Blessed and holy are those who share in the first resurrection. The second death has no power over them, but they will be priests of God and of Christ and will reign

with him for a thousand years." (Revelation 20:4–6)

"On that day living water will flow out from Jerusalem, half of it east to the Dead Sea and half of it west to the Mediterranean Sea, in summer and in winter. The Lord will be king over the whole earth. On that day there will be one Lord, and his name the only name." (Zechariah 14:8–9)

These verses teach us two extremely significant matters. The first is that there must be a literal millennial period between the return of Christ Jesus to Jerusalem and this battle's commencement. We will never see this battle in our lifetimes. The second and more important matter is the imprisonment of Satan during the one thousand years. Due to his imprisonment, he will no longer blind or provoke humanity to sin against God. *This is the crucial point!* After this millennial period, however, something very serious and extraordinary will take place: Satan will be set free to deceive the nations of the world (Revelation 20:7–10). Note the words from Ezekiel:

"This is what the Sovereign Lord says: On that day thoughts will come into your mind and you will devise an evil scheme." (Ezekiel 38:10)

This would not and could not occur if it wasn't for some outside source (Satan) tempting the people to sin. They will succumb accordingly. Having lived in a world free from exposure to evil will be their undoing. But why would God allow this? This is easy to understand as a test. God, for some inexplicable reason, will need to examine and test this generation of people for their faith and character. Genuineness! Again, these words from the prophet Jeremiah:

> *"I the Lord search the heart and examine the mind, to reward each person according to their conduct, according to what their deeds deserve." (Jeremiah 17:10)*

The seriousness of this act of rebellion will cause God to strike these nations with the full force of His vengeance. It will be a literal death penalty. These people, unlike us, will know who God is totally and completely. They will be born into a world where the knowledge of God and His Christ will be everywhere. God will be a living reality before their very eyes. Faith, therefore, will not be a struggle. Sin will be revealed for what it is—disobedience to God. So, what we have here is treason, pure and simple. It's as simple as that. Their guilt and blood will be upon their own heads.

With the release of Satan, mankind will apparently find sin delightful again. Satan's work of temptation (those evil thoughts and plans written about in Ezekiel 38:10) will appeal to these people and nations whom God rightly names Gog and Magog. Understand the extreme importance of this, especially where the nation of Israel is concerned. Gog and Magog will not be destroyed for attacking the nation of Israel, but rather for committing the ultimate of all treasonous acts against Almighty God, the one and only true Father of us all! Christ the King will be in the city of Jerusalem when this goes down. Why else would His Majesty use these words?

> *"...they will know that I am the Lord."*
>
> *(Ezekiel 38:23, 39:6)*

Note well to that everything, as usual, has been written beforehand. We have the end of the story, meaning that God has forewarned us (and them) so that hopefully the people would be educated and prepared in what not to do! Hence the enormous importance of knowing and paying attention to the scriptures:

> *"We also have the prophetic message as something completely reliable, and you will do well to pay attention to it, as to a light shining in a dark place, until the day dawns and the morning star rises in your hearts." (2 Peter 1:19)*

There will be no excuses before God. One is left wondering and questioning about Gog and Magog and their ignorance of the Word of God—and worse, their desire to sin and rebel against Him. Too easy will be their seduction to Satan. This is the real issue here.

The only way I know to understand and explain the why of this is by quoting the words of Christ Jesus Himself:

> *"This is the verdict: Light has come into the world, but people loved darkness instead of light because their deeds were evil. Everyone who does evil hates the light, and*

> *will not come into the light for fear that their deeds will be exposed." (John 3:19–20)*

Do you see what's going on here? This is a test! Pure and simple. Instead of delighting in the Lord and in his Laws, the delight in doing evil will appeal to these people instead. Ultimately, this is the real reason why they will be destroyed, and it will take those living in the land of Israel some seven years to bury the dead, and seven more years to clean the land of their weapons of war (Ezekiel 39:9–16). These weapons, by the way, will not be of the industrial or technological kind, given that the people descend upon the land of Israel on horseback.

> *"You will come from your place in the far north, you and many nations with you, all of them riding on horses, a great horde, a mighty army. You will advance against my people Israel like a cloud that covers the land. In days to come, Gog, I will bring you against my land, so that the nations may know me when I am proved holy through you before their eyes." (Ezekiel 38:15–16)*

Is this not odd? Why would they use horses when we have trains, planes, and automobiles at our disposal? Perhaps, after suffering through Armageddon, the world will revert to a pre-industrial state where agriculture is the main economic driver. The age of oil will be at an end!

When you add it all together, it just doesn't make sense that Gog and Magog could be a reference to Germany and Russia. That's quite an absurd interpretation rather.

Furthermore, consider this! If the current interpretation is true, the logical question is: what could make these nations more deserving of future punishment than what occurred during the First and Second World Wars? What could make a present-day Israel more deserving of heavenly protection than what her children suffered under communism and fascism? God did nothing to stop the horrible crimes of Hitler and Stalin, so why should we believe that in some near future He would? This is utterly preposterous.

Consider this also: according to Ezekiel, these nations attack *"a peaceful and unsuspecting people—all of them living without walls and without gates"* (Ezekiel 38:11). This is quite perplexing, because it implies that the citizens of Jerusalem will be living in such peace and safety that there will be literally nothing to make them afraid—no hatreds of any kind, no terrorism, nothing to bring fear. There will apparently be no need for defences of any kind to protect the people. A military will not exist, nor will an armed populace be needed. What a contrast this is to us today, where nation after nation arms themselves to the teeth with every unimaginable kind of weapon there is, especially where the current nation of Israel is concerned. Travel there and everywhere you go you will find an armed to the teeth populace.

Peace? What peace? An unsuspecting people? Really? There is currently so much suspicion that even children are suspected terrorists. Israel is even currently building its own iron curtain (concrete walls). Consider these words from Ariel Sharon, former Israeli prime minister:

> "Even if you'll prove to me by mathematical means that the present war in Lebanon is a dirty immoral war, I don't care. Moreover, even if you will prove to me that we have not achieved and will not achieve any of our aims in Lebanon, that we will neither create a friendly regime in Lebanon

nor destroy the Syrians or even the PLO, even then I don't care. It was still worth it. Even if Galilee is shelled again by Katyushas in a year's time, I don't really care. We shall start another war, kill and destroy more and more, until they will have had enough.

Tell me, do the baddies of this world have a bad time? If anyone tries to touch them, the evil men cut his hands and legs off. They hunt and catch whatever they feel like eating. They don't suffer from indigestion and are not punished by Heaven. I want Israel to join that club. Maybe the world will then at last begin to fear me instead of feeling sorry for me. Maybe they will start to tremble, to fear my madness instead of admiring my nobility. Thank god for that. Let them tremble, let them call us a mad state. Let them understand that we are a wild country, dangerous to our surroundings, not normal, that we might go crazy if one of our children is murdered—just one! That we might go wild and burn all the oil fields in the Middle East! I... Let them be aware in Washington, Moscow, Damascus and China that if one of our ambassadors is shot, or even a consul or the most junior embassy official, we might start World War Three just like that!

If your nice civilized parents had come here in time instead of writing books about the love for humanity and singing

Hear O Israel on the way to the gas chambers... now don't be shocked, if they instead had killed six million Arabs here or even one million, what would have happened? Sure, two or three nasty pages would have been written in the history books, we would have been called all sorts of names, but we could be here today as a people of 25 million!

Even today I am willing to volunteer to do the dirty work for Israel, to kill as many Arabs as necessary, to deport them, to expel and burn them, to have everyone hate us, to pull the rug from underneath the feet of the Diaspora Jews, so that they will be forced to run to us crying. Even if it means blowing up one or two synagogues here and there, I don't care. And I don't mind if after the job is done you put me in front of a Nuremberg Trial and then jail me for life. Hang me if you want, as a war criminal... What you lot don't understand is that the dirty work of Zionism is not finished yet, far from it." [2]

Peace like what we find written in Ezekiel just doesn't exist, and given the prophecies of Armageddon, how will it? It's hard to understand how Ezekiel 38–39 could have anything to do with our current day and age. We need to be for Christ Jesus, who was worthy to

---

[2] David Duke, "Ariel Sharon: The Terrorist Behind the 9-11 Attack!" May 2, 2004 (http://davidduke.com/ariel-sharon-the-terrorist-behind-the-9-11-attack-3/).

open the final scrolls. Revelation gives us the knowledge we need to make the connection and understand this prophecy.

So, to conclude, the teaching here is that Gog and Magog are the ultimate of all treasonous nations. What an unimaginably dreadful and bloody end this future attack will be under the millennial Kingdom of Christ Jesus. This is the correct interpretation of Ezekiel 38–39 about Gog and Magog. After these events, we will find the creation of a new heaven and a new earth, and a new city of Jerusalem descending out of heaven at the end of recorded time.

> "I saw the Holy City, the new Jerusalem, coming down out of heaven from God, prepared as a bride beautifully dressed for her husband." (Revelation 21:2)

Modern-day Israel, as we can clearly see, has nothing whatsoever to worry or concern itself with where the prophecy of Gog and Magog is concerned, but a question certainly needs to be raised about the current malaise in the Middle East. Indeed, is what we're witnessing in the Middle East today just a self-fulfilling prophecy? That's the important question. Yes, that does appear to be the case. The present crisis never would have occurred if only the Jewish people along with a major portion of the Christian Church had accepted what the scriptures prophesy about the Savior Christ Jesus and began with Him accordingly. This is especially the case where C. I. Scofield is concerned. It is a mistake the likes of which is leading to what the bible refers to as the Abomination of Desolation and Armageddon ultimately! They should never have rejected this Christ for an impostor who is no doubt about to make its presence known in the City of Jerusalem!

Considering this, it must be wondered why anyone would want to live there, or anywhere in proximity to it. Take, for example, the scriptures about an earthquake hitting Jerusalem and killing some seven thousand people. Why would people want to live there?

> "At that very hour there was a severe earthquake and a tenth of the city collapsed. Seven thousand people were killed in the earthquake, and the survivors were terrified and gave glory to the God of heaven." (Revelation 11:13)

Far more frightening is this scripture:

> "So, when you see standing in the holy place "the abomination that causes desolation," spoken of through the prophet Daniel—let the reader understand—then let those who are in Judea flee to the mountains. Let no one on the housetop go down to take anything out of the house. Let no one in the field go back to get their cloak. How dreadful it will be in those days for pregnant women and nursing mothers! Pray that your flight will not take place in winter or on the Sabbath. For then there will be great distress, unequaled from the beginning of the world until now—and never to be equaled again.

> *If those days had not been cut short, no one would survive, but for the sake of the elect those days will be shortened." (Matthew 24:15–22)*

Why would God bring about the rebirth of a nation only to see her capital city destroyed? You know, just because the Bible prophesies something doesn't mean that God wanted it that way. I want the reader to understand here the grave seriousness of this interpretation of Gog and Magog, because the insinuation by teachers like Scofield and his dispensationalism is that God has a plan and purpose for Israel's rebirth. This is not true! If God wanted a nation rebirth, He could have done it without so much as a drop of blood. Scofield and Darby blew it with their interpretation. Dr. Lutzweiler had it correct what we have in dispensationalism is a dual covenant theology which is wrong, and it needs to be repudiated. Where the Jerusalem Declaration on Christian Zionism is concerned, then they are correct that a "political/military program has replaced the teachings of Christ."[3] I think that is truly frightening, something for which God will surely visit and judge the Church. Is this not the precursor to the Abomination of Desolation? What then should be the proper response of Christians to Israel?

At the walls of Jericho, Joshua had an interesting encounter with God's messengers. He asked them if they were for him or for his enemies. The angels replied that they were neither for them, nor for him, but for the Lord (Joshua 5:14). That should be the response of every Christian toward Israel. It would keep one's hands innocent and clean from bloodshed. Christian Zionism is not healthy or good. Moreover, didn't St. Paul make it abundantly clear that Israel had become a hybrid plant? (Romans 11:17–19) The natural branches were broken off (God breaking His covenant with the natural children which God declared

---

[3]*The Holy Land Christian Ecumenical Foundation,* "The Jerusalem Declaration on Christian Zionism." Accessed: September 1, 2016 (http://hcef.org/1694-the-jerusalem-declaration-on-christian-zionism/).

back in Zechariah 11) and we were grafted in. God's promises to Israel were conditional (Deuteronomy 11:26) and Israel accordingly became something entirely different.

> *"Therefore, I tell you that the kingdom of God will be taken away from you and given to a people who will produce its fruit."*
> *(Matthew 21:43)*

> *"No, a person is a Jew who is one inwardly; and circumcision is circumcision of the heart, by the Spirit, not by the written code. Such a person's praise is not from other people, but from God." (Romans 2:29)*

Does this mean that the Church is the Israel of God? Well, there is certainly a good argument to be made for going in that direction. It was the historic position of the Church Universal, and it should have remained so.

Knowing all this beforehand then, is it not the Christian duty to warn people of the coming disaster and catastrophe? Is it not the Christian duty to fully educate the people of the impending arrival of the antichrist? Is it not our duty to try and save people?

So, to close out this chapter, it would be good to hear the words of Dr. Oscar Levy. The Christian Church has made a very serious mistake and is guilty by both association (Christian Zionism)[4] in having misinterpreted Holy Scripture, a mistake which will surely go down in

---

[4] *YouTube*, "Noam Chomsky—Why does the U.S. Support Israel?" July 2, 2016 (https://youtu.be/lUQ_oMubbcM).

history as one of the biggest blunders of biblical exegesis ever made, period.

> "We (Jews) have erred, my friend; we have most grievously erred. And if there was truth in our error 3,000, 2,000, nay, 100 years ago, there is now nothing but falseness and madness... a madness that will produce an even greater misery and an even wider anarchy.
>
> I confess it to you, openly and sincerely, and with a sorrow whose depth and pain an ancient Psalmist, and only he, could moan into this burning universe of ours...
>
> We who have posed as the saviours of the world; we who have even boasted of having given it "the" Saviour; we are today nothing else but the world's seducers, its destroyers, its incendiaries, its executioners. We who have promised to lead you to a new Heaven, we have finally succeeded in leading you into a new Hell...
>
> There has been no progress, least of all moral progress... And it is just our Morality, which has prohibited all real progress, and—
>
> what is worse—which even stands in the way of every future and natural reconstruction in this ruined world of ours... I look at this world, and I shudder at its

ghastliness; I shudder all the more as I know the spiritual authors of all this ghastliness..."[5]

---

[5] http://www.sweetliberty.org/issues/israel/levy.htm

Chapter Three - The Great Heresy?

> "Then the survivors from all the nations that have attacked Jerusalem will go up year after year to worship the King, the Lord Almighty, and to celebrate the Festival of Tabernacles. If any of the peoples of the earth do not go up to Jerusalem to worship the King, the Lord Almighty, they will have no rain. If the Egyptian people do not go up and take part, they will have no rain. The Lord will bring on them the plague he inflicts on the nations that do not go up to celebrate the Festival of Tabernacles." (Zechariah 14:16–18)

This thesis might come as a shock to a great many people who think that it's a new teaching that has never existed before. In some ways, that could very well be the case. With forty years in the church I have never come across this material from any source apart from reading it in the Bible itself and learning about it through my own prayers.

As for the idea that Christ will rule for an actual millennium, that was discovered by the Church father's millennia ago. It's called the doctrine of Chiliasm, and incredibly, it was condemned by the Church fathers at the Council of Nicaea as heretical. This is hard to understand. Even harder to understand is how anyone could interpret the many episodes in the book of Revelation as just a mystical spiritual event that has no relation to the carnal world. As we have clearly seen, and will see again in numerous illustrations to follow, everything about the prophecies of the book of Revelation has consequences for the carnal world. This is especially the case where the Feast of Tabernacles is concerned.

It's a shame that earlier Church leaders didn't discover these truths, because they could have saved us all a terrible amount of confusion, and possibly prevented much of what is currently happening in the Middle East. Chiliasm will be proven correct.

Before we go there, however, let's stop here and look at the portion of scripture talking about rain and the Feast of Tabernacles. This right here reveals just how very serious the people's treason is.

It is amazing—amazing, in fact—to read about rain in the prophecy of Zechariah and how if anyone doesn't attend an annual feast in Jerusalem during the reign of Christ Jesus, no rain will fall upon their respective lands. What exactly is this all about and why would it have anything to do with the Feast of Tabernacles?

Of all the feasts that the nation of Israel was called upon to celebrate, the Feast of Tabernacles is most interesting because it deals with thanksgiving. Shouldn't a people be thankful? Most certainly. This was especially the case for Israel. After having been delivered from slavery under an Egyptian Pharaoh to a land they could call their own, they were a free and happy people. The Feast of Tabernacles was first instituted by God in Exodus 23 under Moses (1706 B.C.) to be a celebration for all things agricultural. It was celebrated for an entire week from Tishri 15-22, which corresponds to October, the month of harvest.

> *"Celebrate the Festival of Harvest with the first fruits of the crops you sow in your field. Celebrate the Festival of Ingathering at the end of the year, when you gather in your crops from the field." (Exodus 23:16)*

A nation's lifeblood is its agriculture.

> "Cultivators of the earth are the most valuable citizens. They are the most vigorous, the most independent, the most virtuous, and they are tied to their country, and wedded to its liberty and interests by the most lasting bonds... I consider the class of artificers as the panders of vice, and the instruments by which the liberties of a country are overturned... I think our governments will remain virtuous for many centuries; as long as they are chiefly agricultural."[6]
>
> —Thomas Jefferson

When Israel was living in Egypt, this constituted a great deal of hard labour in that all watering had to be done by hand. In the Promised Land, however, this was not the case at all. Rather, water came by way of rain from heaven. God wanted the people to understand this and promised that if the people loved and obeyed Him wholeheartedly, He would make sure their land would never suffer from droughts.

> *"Observe therefore all the commands I am giving you today, so that you may have the strength to go in and take over the land that you are crossing the Jordan to possess, and so that you may live long in the land the Lord swore to your ancestors to give to them*

---

[6] Daniel Lattier, *Intellectual Takeout*, "When Fewer Men Farm, a Civilization Dies." August 16, 2016 (http://www.intellectualtakeout.org/blog/when-fewer-men-farm-civilization-dies).

and their descendants, a land flowing with milk and honey. The land you are entering to take over is not like the land of Egypt, from which you have come, where you planted your seed and irrigated it by foot as in a vegetable garden. But the land you are crossing the Jordan to take possession of is a land of mountains and valleys that drinks rain from heaven. It is a land the Lord your God cares for; the eyes of the Lord your God are continually on it from the beginning of the year to its end.

So if you faithfully obey the commands I am giving you today—to love the Lord your God and to serve him with all your heart and with all your soul—then I will send rain on your land in its season, both autumn and spring rains, so that you may gather in your grain, new wine and olive oil. I will provide grass in the fields for your cattle, and you will eat and be satisfied.

Be careful, or you will be enticed to turn away and worship other gods and bow down to them. Then the Lord's anger will burn against you, and he will shut up the

> *heavens so that it will not rain and the ground will yield no produce, and you will soon perish from the good land the Lord is giving you." (Deuteronomy 11:8–17)*

We need to be hydrated through rain, so imagine what this was like for Israel! The weather was no longer a happenstance, a force of nature. God linked the nation's faithfulness to Him by way of climate change. For an agricultural society, this should have married the concepts of faithfulness and provision forever. Add to this the timing of the Israelites' delivery from bondage and their entering into the Promised Land, for the celebration of the Feast of Tabernacles in September/October, couldn't have been more perfect.

What we have here is thanksgiving coupled with remembrance, and it was commanded by God to be celebrated in tents or booths among the fields, away from the people's homes, this for an entire week. It was a celebration of everything God had done for the nation and was continuing to do.

Isn't this remarkable? It reveals that faith is not blind at all. God can indeed be observed to exist. Living under such knowledge and blessings is the pinnacle of life. To enjoy the presence of God and His faithfulness is the greatest thing a people, any people, could experience.

During the golden age to come, we will all experience this reality. All the prophets knew and understood this. Samuel, after suffering with the children of Israel, and after they asked for a king to rule over them in place of God, wrote:

> *"Now then, stand still and see this great thing the Lord is about to do before your eyes! Is it not wheat harvest now? I will call on the Lord to send thunder and rain. And you will realize what an evil thing you*

did in the eyes of the Lord when you asked for a king.

Then Samuel called on the Lord, and that same day the Lord sent thunder and rain. So, all the people stood in awe of the Lord and of Samuel." (1 Samuel 12:16–18)

As a nation, Israel truly had it all. This kind of weather phenomena occurred in practically every generation. Theologically speaking, it's referred to as divine communication. For a God, what better way is there to communicate than by using the weather? Droughts especially became a source of chastisement and discipline. Every generation to some degree has experienced this. Again, consider the words by Israel's most famous leaders:

"The poor and needy search for water, but there is none; their tongues are parched with thirst. But I the Lord will answer them; I, the God of Israel, will not forsake them. I will make rivers flow on barren heights, and springs within the valleys. I will turn the desert into pools of water, and the parched ground into springs. I will put in the desert the cedar and the acacia, the myrtle and the olive. I will set junipers in the wasteland, the fir and the cypress together, so that people

may see and know, may consider and understand, that the hand of the Lord has done this, that the Holy One of Israel has created it." (Isaiah 41:17–20)

This is what the Lord Almighty says: "These people say, 'The time has not yet come to rebuild the Lord's house.

Then the word of the Lord came through the prophet Haggai: "Is it a time for you yourselves to be living in your panelled houses, while this house remains a ruin?"

Now this is what the Lord Almighty says: "Give careful thought to your ways. You have planted much but harvested little. You eat, but never have enough. You drink, but never have your fill. You put on clothes but are not warm. You earn wages, only to put them in a purse with holes in it."

This is what the Lord Almighty says: "Give careful thought to your ways. Go up into the mountains and bring down timber and build my house, so that I may take pleasure in it and be honored," says the Lord. "You expected much, but see, it turned out to be little. What you brought home, I blew away. Why?" declares the Lord Almighty. "Because of my house, which remains a ruin, while each of you is busy with your own house. Therefore, because of you the heavens have withheld their dew and the earth its crops. I called for a drought on the fields and the mountains, on the grain, the new wine, the olive oil and everything else the ground produces, on people and livestock, and on all the labor of your hands." (Haggai 1:2–11, emphasis added)

King Solomon though sums it up best at the dedication of the Temple:

"When the heavens are shut up and there is no rain because your people have sinned against you, and when they pray toward this place and give praise to your name and turn from their sin because you have afflicted them, then hear from heaven and forgive the sin of your servants, your people Israel. Teach them the right way to live and send rain on the land you gave your people for an inheritance." (2 Chronicles 6:26–27)

God's promises to Israel were conditional. Much can be said and gleaned from Israel's history regarding climate change.[7] To discover the solution to all our weathers woes today, which is surely the work of God, one need only read and pay attention to these words from Amos:

> *"I also withheld rain from you when the harvest was still three months away. I sent rain on one town but withheld it from another. One field had rain; another had none and dried up. People staggered from town to town for water but did not get enough to drink, yet you have not returned to me,"* declares the Lord. (Amos 4:7–8, emphasis added)

So, the next time you hear scientists saying that they don't understand certain abrupt meteorological events, simply point them in the direction of the Bible. Perhaps then we'll gain some closure to the issues of climate change. If perchance there are some who read this and say to themselves, *This is just biblical fables,* take a read at what archaeology has discovered:

> "Climate during the past 11,000 years was long believed to have been uneventful, but paleoclimatic records increasingly demonstrate climatic instability.

---

[7] For more on this subject, see my book entitled *Climate Change the Work of God*.

Multidecadal-to multicentury-length droughts started abruptly, were unprecedented in the experience of the existing societies, and were highly disruptive to their agricultural foundations because social and technological innovations were not available to counter the rapidity, amplitude, and duration of changing climatic conditions...

In the Middle East, a ~200 year drought forced the abandonment of agricultural settlements in the Levant and northern Mesopotamia. The subsequent return to moister conditions in Mesopotamia promoted settlement of the Tigris-Euphrates alluvial plain and delta, where breachable river levees and seasonal basins may have encouraged early Mesopotamia irrigation agriculture. By 3500 B.C. urban Late Urak society flourished in southern Mesopotamia, sustained by a system of high yield cereal irrigation agriculture with efficient canal transport. Late Urak "colony" settlements were founded across the dry-farming portions of the Near East. But these colonies and the expansion of Late Urak society collapsed suddenly at about 3200 to 3500 B.C. Archaeologists have puzzled over this collapse for the past 30 years. Now there are hints in the paleoclimatic record that it may be related to a short (less than 200 year) but severe drought...

Following the return to wetter conditions politically centralized and class-based urban societies emerged and expanded across the riverine and dry-farming landscapes of the Mediterranean, Egypt, and West Africa. The Akkadian empire of Mesopotamia, the pyramid constructing Old Kingdom civilization of Egypt, the Harrapan C3 civilization of the Indus valley, and the Early Bronze III civilization of Palestine, Greece, and Crete all reached their economic peak at about 2300 B.C. This period was abruptly terminated before 2200 B.C. by catastrophic drought and cooling that generated regional abandonment, collapse, and habitat-tracking. Paleo-climatic data from numerous sites document changes in the Mediterranean westerlies and monsoon rainfall during this event, with precipitation reductions of up to 30% that diminished agricultural production from the Aegean to the Indus."[8]

What profound statements to make regarding something that's at the very heart of what the Bible has been saying? What an incredible

---

[8] Harvey Weiss and Richard S. Bradley, "What Drives Societal Collapse," *Science* (January 26, 2001): 609–610.

resemblance, if not outright corroboration and substantiation, of the Bible. This is what happened to such nations as the Hittites, Amorites, Edomites, Assyrians, Philistines, Israelites, and Egyptian kingdoms. The biblical accounts of these nations' weather-related demises are quite graphic. If one needs more from the Bible, consider these further words in relation to the house of Israel from the sixth century B.C:

> *"When I shoot at you with my deadly and destructive arrows of famine, I will shoot to destroy you. I will bring more and more famine upon you and cut off your supply of food. I will send famine and wild beasts against you, and they will leave you childless. Plague and bloodshed will sweep through you, and I will bring the sword against you. I the Lord have spoken." (Ezekiel 5:16–17)*

> *"The word of the Lord came to me: "Son of man, if a country sins against me by being unfaithful and I stretch out my hand against it to cut off its food supply and send famine upon it and kill its people and their animals, even if these three men—Noah, Daniel and Job—were in it, they could save only themselves by their righteousness, declares the Sovereign Lord." (Ezekiel 14:12–14)*

When you add it all together, you can see a story of climate change so far from what we're being told today that it must be wondered: why has no one been teaching this? This is especially true of the Jewish people, particularly their rabbinical priesthood. If anyone should be teaching the world the truth about climate change, it should be them.

Again, the Bible has much more to teach on this important and vital subject. In fact, the book of Job alone lays the foundation for understanding everything about global warming. Job is the premier meteorologist of the Bible. And lastly, we mustn't forget the Christian Church. As the engrafted branch into the olive tree called Israel (Romans 11), we find ourselves experiencing climatological events that are truly a wonder to behold.

Consider the following story from Basil Miller's book about Charles Finney:

> "During the summer of 1853 Oberlin was struck with a severe drought. The hay fields were dried up so there was no feed for the cattle. The cattle soon must die and the harvest fail unless rain comes. Crops had withered, wells dried up, and the parched earth became powdery.
>
> On Sunday morning the church was filled. Not a cloud was in sight and no one expected a drop of water to fall from the skies that day. The situation was desperate. Finney arose from his chair walked to the pulpit and lifted his voice in prayer.
>
> "O Lord! Send us rain. We pray for rain. Our harvests perish. There is not a drop for the thirsting birds. The ground is parched. The choking cattle lift their voices toward a brassy heaven and lowing, cry

'Lord give us water... We do not presume to dictate to Thee what is best for us, yet Thou dost invite us to come to Thee as children to a father and tell Thee all our wants. We want rain! Even the squirrels in the woods are suffering for want of it. Unless Thou givest us rain our cattle must die... O Lord, send us rain! and send it now! For Jesus sake!' Amen."

"In the preachers voice," reports the California minister, "was the plaintiveness of a creatures cry. I do not know whether any pencil caught more of this wonderful prayer, but all who heard it had to tell of its bold importunity. It had the pathos and power of an Isaiah."

Then the pastor-revivalist poured out his soul in a searching sermon, "hewing close to the line," from the text, "I have somewhat against thee because thou hast left thy first love."

"Not many minutes did the sermon go on before a cloud about the size of a man's hand came athwart the summer sky," says the California preacher. "It grew fast. The wind rattled the shutters of the old church. Darkness came on the air, joy aroused our anxious hearts as great raindrops pattered on the sun-scorched shingles of the monumental old church. Finney's lithe figure, tall as a Sioux warrior, ruddy as a David, trembled. His clarion voice choked. God had heard his cry. The sermon was never finished, for torrents of water poured from the prayer-unlocked heavens. The preacher bowed over the pulpit and said, Let us thank the Lord for the rain."

He gave out the hymn, When all they mercies, O my God my rising soul surveys, Transported with the view, I'm lost in wonder, love and praise.

The congregation could not sing for weeping. Then Finney lifted heavenward a prayer of thanksgiving and praise. "I can remember not a word of the closing prayer, but the reverent and relaxed figure, the pathetic voice, the pallid and awe-struck countenance, are vivid as if it was yesterday; the plank sidewalks of the dear old town splashed our garments as we walked home from a short service, of which life's memory must be lasting." This is the testimony of the student who sat in the gallery and saw and heard Finney that morning."[9]

Another example is what occurred in America with Oberlin College under the leadership of Asa Mahan:

"I had an appointment," he said, "during the season of afflictive drought, to

---

[9] Basil Miller, *Charles Finney* (Minneapolis, MN: Zondervan Publishing House, 1941), 126–128.

preach in one of the churches of the city where I lived one Sabbath morning. As we came to our carriage, I said to my wife, 'There is not the remotest probability that it will rain today. I will, therefore, carry in the robe which we usually take with us,' and did so.

"When I kneeled before that congregation, I had no more expectation that it would rain that day outside than inside the house of God. When I began to pray about the drought, however a power came over me which rendered that prayer a wonder to myself and the congregation. The Monday's issue of our daily paper contained this statement: 'The preacher in one of our churches prayed very fervently yesterday morning that it might rain, and his congregation were drenched with rain on going home at the close of that service.'

"I can never tell when then 'spirit of grace and of supplication,' in that form, shall be poured upon me. Nor do I feel under obligation to have such experience whenever I pray. All that I can do, or feel bound to do, is leave my heart open, and let the Spirit intercede in it as and when He chooses. This I do say, however, that when the Spirit does thus intercede, I always obtain the specific object for which I pray. Nor can anyone pray under the intercessory power of the Spirit without the hearer, as well as himself, marking the peculiarity of prayer.

"Hence it is that, for many years past, my students, in times of drought, for example, have been accustomed to say, 'We shall have rain now. Did you mark our President's prayer?' Nor were they ever disappointed."[10]

Also consider the story of the Methodist Church in England under the leadership of John Wesley:

"Monday, 17. As we were walking toward Wapping, the rain poured down with such violence that we were obliged to take shelter till it abated. We then held on to Gravel Lane, in many parts of which the waters were like a river. However, we got on pretty well till the rain put out the candle in our lantern. We then were obliged to wade through all, till we came to the chapel yard. Just as we entered, a little streak of lightning appeared in the southwest. There was likewise a small clap of thunder and a vehement burst of rain, which rushed so plentifully through our shattered tiles that the vestry was all in a float. Soon after I began reading prayers, the lightning flamed all around it, and the thunder rolled over our heads. When it grew louder and louder,

---

[10] Edwin and Lillian Harvest, *How They Prayed* (Shoals, IN: Old Path Tracts Society, 1987), 74-75.

> perceiving many of the strangers to be much affrighted, I broke off the prayers after the collect, "Lighten our darkness, we beseech thee, O Lord," and began applying, "The Lord sitteth above the water flood; the Lord remaineth a king forever" (Ps. 29:10) Presently the lightning, thunder, and rain ceased, and we had a remarkably calm evening. It was observed that exactly at this hour they were acting Mac Beth in Drury Lane, and just as the mock thunder began, the Lord began to thunder out of heaven. For a while it put them to a stand; but they soon took courage and went on. Otherwise it might have been suspected that the fear of God had crept into the very theater!"[11]

Next, consider what occurred over Singapore in the early 1980s:

> "Last year, the business leaders of Singapore got a vision from the Holy Spirit. They were to sponsor a national crusade to reach all of Singapore. They rented the local soccer stadium, which seats 70,000 people. One business leader alone, Mr. Wy Wy Wong, paid for the total advertising in every newspaper in the country. The committee was composed of pastors, professional people and businessmen. These men and

---

[11] *Christian Classics Ethereal Library*, "The Journal of John Wesley." Date of access: June 29, 2016 (https://www.ccel.org/ccel/wesley/journal.vi.x.ix.html).

women had one thing in common. They had a burning desire for revival in Singapore, which had a small Christian population. Night after night, for five straight nights, the rain came in torrents. But by six o'clock every evening, the sky would clear and we were able to have large crowds gather to hear the gospel. The total count of people that came forward to accept Christ amazed me. I repeated nightly. "Please only those who want to accept Christ as their personal Savior for the first time in your life, only you come forward." Yet, we counted more than 50,000 people making decisions for Christ."[12]

What a truly fascinating and amazing God we serve.

There is more to tell, but what does any of this have to do with the prophecy of Gog and Magog? Everything, of course. As Zechariah points out, no rain will fall upon the people and nations that refuse to attend a thanksgiving event in Jerusalem. Why? Christ's salvation deserves a celebration of thanksgiving on a global scale. That God would connect this celebration to the harvest proves His magnificent and wondrous ways!

Do you see then just how serious and blatant a treasonous act of sin their actions will be? No one will be innocent of the destruction raining down upon these people. They will deserve exactly what they get. I want the reader to understand that many nations in the Old Testament, including Israel, were just as guilty of similar sins of treason; unlike us, they knew God existed and yet chose to follow idols. That's why no scripture is more important to heed today than this one:

---

[12] P.Y. Cho, *More Than Numbers* (Milton Keynes, UK: Word Publishing, 1984), 130.

> "How much more severely do you think someone deserves to be punished who has trampled the Son of God underfoot, who has treated as an unholy thing the blood of the covenant that sanctified them, and who has insulted the Spirit of grace?" (Hebrews 10:29)

And of course, this one:

> "See to it that you do not refuse him who speaks. If they did not escape when they refused him who warned them on earth, how much less will we, if we turn away from him who warns us from heaven? At that time his voice shook the earth, but now he has promised, "Once more I will shake not only the earth but also the heavens." The words "once more" indicate the removing of what can be shaken—that is, created things—so that what cannot be shaken may remain.
> Therefore, since we are receiving a kingdom that cannot be shaken, let us be thankful, and so worship God acceptably with reverence and awe, for our "God is a consuming fire." (Hebrews 12:25)

A consuming fire is exactly what Gog and Magog will receive—and Satan will receive his final home in the lake of fire!

That brings us to the end of this thesis, but I'd like to mention one last thing which brings tears to my eyes: The Feast of Tabernacles is also a birthday party. Yes, a birthday party! Contrary to what we've all been brought up to believe, Christ Jesus was not born on December 25. He was born during the first week of October. How do we know that? According to Dr. David Lutzweiler, we need only look at Luke 3:23 and Christ's baptism by John, which occurred when *"Jesus himself was about thirty years old."* We know that Christ's public ministry occurred over a period of three and a half years, so considering that His crucifixion happened at Passover, at the end of March or the first week of April, we can subtract six months to find the approximate time of his birth: the end of September or beginning of October. Therefore, Christ Jesus' birthday is around October 1. That is astounding, and how typical of God to time it during the harvest. The Bread from Heaven was born during the harvest season! Nothing could be more perfect.[13]

The Feast of Tabernacles then isn't only a celebration of remembrance and thanksgiving, but a birthday party as well. This is utterly spectacular. Going by Christ's birth date, we can place the immaculate conception at the beginning of the year, around January 1. What a truly fascinating God we serve. Is it any wonder then that God would make it a requirement that such a feast—and only this feast, a birthday party for all eternity—be celebrated by all peoples of the world throughout the millennial period? Wow!

> *"Then the survivors from all the nations that have attacked Jerusalem will go up year after year to worship the King, the Lord Almighty, and to celebrate the Festival of Tabernacles. If any of the peoples of the earth do not go up to Jerusalem to worship*

---

[13] Dr. David Lutzweiler, "How We Know the Birthday of Jesus." Date of access: August 22, 2016.
ttps://docs.wixstatic.com/ugd/a1b4f0_5f2d3dbdbe1d44a99aa1f6488ee0e627.pdf

> *the King, the Lord Almighty, they will have no rain. If the Egyptian people do not go up and take part, they will have no rain. The Lord will bring on them the plague he inflicts on the nations that do not go up to celebrate the Festival of Tabernacles." (Zechariah 14:16–18}*

True to God's words, mankind will not live by bread alone, but by every word that proceeds from the mouth of Almighty God. This is so magnificent in scope. How interesting it is that the apostle John concludes, with his vision of God's glory in a new heaven and new earth, that which Ezekiel prophesied as ending Israel's long exile. While it will be glorious, unfortunately it won't happen in our lifetimes but rather at least a thousand years from now. The new Jerusalem will radiate God's magnificent glory forever and ever! And note that this is upon the earth and not just in heaven, as though we are to just spiritualize the words of Revelation 20 as the Church fathers were wont to do.

Whoever would have thought that studying the Feast of Tabernacles and climate change, of all things, would take us right into the future history of our world? With the God of the Bible, though, that's the way it is. He made it abundantly clear for all to see and read:

> *"I am God, and there is no other; I am God, and there is none like me. I make known the end from the beginning, from ancient times, what is still to come. I say, "My purpose will stand, and I will do all that I please." (Isaiah 46: 9–10)*

This matter was reiterated by Christ Jesus, who likewise revealed the same abilities:

> *"I have told you now before it happens,*
> *so that when it does happen you will believe."*
> (John 14:29)

So, prophecy must begin with Christ Jesus in the book of Revelation. Wow! Israel is in for an interesting future, if not a difficult one. Given what the words of God say, this future could have been prevented if only they had paid attention to everything God said to them. This is especially true where climate change is concerned. As we have seen, Israel's history winds its way through practically every generation. Even today, not much has changed. Rainwater is still a scarce commodity. So scarce, in fact, that wars have been fought over what little remains. The Dead Sea and the Sea of Galilee are in fact literally drying up! Amazing. How can it be, in a land where practically everyone believes in God, that nobody can make the connection that this is a direct result of God? {Deuteronomy 11:8–17} Have things really gone so far that even today people in the holy land—and not just Jews and Moslems but Christians as well—have been deceived into believing what science must say regarding the weather, that it is just a natural process, ruled by the law of physics?

Apparently so, except for one rather interesting individual. I heard a report on the radio that said he was yelling to the people in the streets of Baghdad. He was shouting, and I paraphrase, "Hey! Look what God is doing to the American forces!" Upon hearing this, I immediately went to get a copy of a newspaper to learn exactly what this individual was referring to. I then came across a truly fascinating and eye-opening report and read.

When Bravo Company was some twenty-five miles from Baghdad, they were stopped dead by a series of storms that sprang up out of nowhere. The day had begun calmly enough, weather wise, but as they neared the city, they encountered a wind sandstorm so fierce that it obscured the sun, turning the desert black. The wind was so strong that it battered and shook their tanks and personnel carriers. After several hours of this, the windstorm turned into a hailstorm with accompanying thunder and lightning. It turned the sand into mud, completely bogging down their vehicles and stalling their advance. They even had to deal with the forming of a lake which almost swamped their vehicles.[14] Can you imagine?

So, everything we have been discussing in this chapter can be seen in our daily headlines. It took a citizen of Baghdad, and a Moslem no less, to recognize it for what it was: a deliberate act of Almighty God. He, of all people, could see what others could not due not to his education in the bible or the Koran —if, that is, there's anything in that book regarding the weather but rather to his acclimatization to that environment. Who lives to see in a desert environment such weather phenomena? It must have been quite the scene from afar, a wind sandstorm with accompanying thunder and then a hailstorm directly over an approaching army division of tanks and personnel carriers in the middle of a desert mere miles away from a city? An incident will no doubt engender a great many questions and concerns about what's happening not only in Iraq but around the entire world.

> *"The Lord will cause people to hear his majestic voice and will make them see his arm coming down with raging anger and consuming fire, with cloudburst, thunderstorm and hail." (Isaiah 30:30)*

Alarming, isn't it? What an example we have here of what will to happen to Gog and Magog. The proof is there for all to see and read.
Christ Jesus is Lord to the glory of God the Father!

---

[14] Matthew Fisher, "Bravo Company and an Embedded...", *Vancouver Sun* (March 26, 2003): A4.

Chapter Four - A Final Proof, The River of Living Water

> "On that day living water will flow out from Jerusalem, half of it east to the Dead Sea and half of it west to the Mediterranean Sea, in summer and in winter."
> (Zechariah 14:8)

Prophecy must correlate between the Old and New Testaments. There can be no argument about this, and working backwards from the end to the beginning has provided some remarkable insights, hasn't it? We see things we have never seen before.

One of the last things that deserves attention is the river of living water that's going to flow from the city of Jerusalem at the time of Christ's return (Zechariah 14). Why? What's significant about that? Water is vital to life and living, and the book of Revelation says that a judgment of God is coming to planet earth in truly horrific ways. All water is to be destroyed because of mankind's lack of repentance and the suffering inflicted upon His people.

> *"The second angel poured out his bowl on the sea, and it turned into blood like that of a dead person, and every living thing in the sea died.*
>
> *The third angel poured out his bowl on the rivers and springs of water, and they*

> *became blood. Then I heard the angel in charge of the waters say: "You are just in these judgments, O Holy One, you who are and who were; for they have shed the blood of your holy people and your prophets, and you have given them blood to drink as they deserve."*
>
> *And I heard the altar respond: "Yes, Lord God Almighty, true and just are your judgments." (Revelation 16:3–7)*

Unfortunately, mankind is going to pay a terrible price for rejecting Christ Jesus in favour of an impostor, the antichrist. Imagine what the world is going to look like with practically all its water resources destroyed? This raises profound questions. For example, will the oceans become so dry that practically all ships that sunk to watery graves be uncovered? Are the dead and dying places of the world going to look like the Grand Canyon of Arizona—or better yet, the Aral Sea or Lake Chad?[15]

Will the survivors of Armageddon be able to make their own journeys among the ruined carcasses of our industrial/technological society? Apparently so! The Bible also mentions earthquakes, and one that will reduce all the cities of the world to rubble. This should remind one of the earthquake storms that hit the Mediterranean basin during the concluding decade of the Roman Empire.

Imagine this is what the world will look like at the return of Christ Jesus to Jerusalem. What needs to happen then for Christ Jesus to take over the political reins of the world and begin to restore things? Well, water will be needed, because life can't live or flourish without it.

---

[15] Shea Gunther, *Mother Nature Network*, "8 Lakes and River that Are Drying Up." May 20, 2016 (http://www.mnn.com/earth-matters/wilderness-resources/photos/7-lakes-and-rivers-that-are-drying-up/bone-dry).

For Zechariah to mention the waters of life therefore is only logical, not to mention important to millennialism. What is not logical, however, is that it flows out of the City of Jerusalem, a city that has little to no waters currently. So, with Christ's return, something changes whereby Jerusalem becomes the healing centre of the world. This only reinforces what we already know, that a Kingdom age lasting an entire millennium will occur.

Conclusion - The Errors of Our Ways

"Do your best to present yourself to God as one approved, a worker who does not need to be ashamed and who correctly handles the word of truth." (2 Timothy 2:15)

I'd like to include some last words concerning Chiliasm. It's hard to understand how the early Church fathers could have condemned Chiliasm, such an important doctrine in the bible, as heretical at the Council of Nicaea. The idea of spiritualizing Revelation 20, meaning that its words are supposed to be symbolic of the eternal glory the church will receive in the other world, makes little sense when we read about the resurrection from the dead.

"I saw thrones on which were seated those who had been given authority to judge. And I saw the souls of those who had been beheaded because of their testimony about Jesus and because of the word of God. They had not worshiped the beast or its image and had not received its mark on their foreheads or their hands. They came to life and reigned with Christ a thousand years. (The rest of the dead did not come to life until the thousand

years were ended.) This is the first resurrection." (Revelation 20:4-6)

How could anyone just spiritualize this? It's talking about the dead and the living by way of a resurrection. Just because you don't understand something doesn't mean you can explain it away by what you do understand, or what you think you understand. Like for example, the kingdom of heaven is within you (Luke 17:20-23). Unfortunately, the idea that martyrs for Christ were to be brought to life with Christ to resume their normal lives in an earthly kingdom was simply too bizarre for many Christians to accept. What did they forget about this?

"...and the tombs broke open. The bodies of many holy people who had died were raised to life. They came out of the tombs after Jesus' resurrection and went into the holy city and appeared to many people." (Matthew 27:52-53)

Is this not a perfect illustration of what St. Paul said regarding how the body must put on immortality? (1 Corinthians 15:53) Revelation 20:4-6 teaches that at Christ's second coming, He will return to the City of Jerusalem for good and resume a normal life along with the resurrected. Will this mean the tens of thousands upon tens of thousands from every age? That's a difficult question which I don't have an exact answer for, except to say that if we take Revelation 20 literally, then the only ones who will reign with Christ will be those who live, suffer, and die during the antichrist's rule:

> *"They had not worshiped the beast or its image and had not received its mark on their foreheads or their hands." (Revelation 20:4)*

Rewarding His people for faithfulness is a concept of God, and maybe each generation receives rewards according to their obedience to God!

> *"Look, I am coming soon! My reward is with me, and I will give to each person according to what they have done."*
> *(Revelation 22:12)*

So, will being faithful even unto death during mankind's darkest period, the tribulation, have its own special rewards? Perhaps. Furthermore, we have the scriptures from Revelation 5:10 and 11:15 respectively:

> *"You have made them to be a kingdom and priests to serve our God, and they will reign on the earth."*
>
> *"The seventh angel sounded his trumpet, and there were loud voices in heaven, which said: "The kingdom of the world has become the kingdom of our Lord*

and of his Messiah, and he will reign for ever and ever."

Likewise, we have from the Old Testament the same kind of sentiment, which is also a prophecy of Christ the Messiah from Bethlehem:

> *"My heart is stirred by a noble theme*
> *as I recite my verses for the king;*
> *my tongue is the pen of a skillful writer.*
> *You are the most excellent of men*
> *and your lips have been anointed with grace,*
> *since God has blessed you forever.*
> *Gird your sword on your side, you mighty one;*
> *clothe yourself with splendor and majesty.*
> *In your majesty ride forth victoriously*
> *in the cause of truth, humility and justice;*
> *let your right hand achieve awesome deeds.*

Let your sharp arrows pierce the hearts of the king's enemies;

    let the nations fall beneath your feet.

Your throne, O God, will last for ever and ever;

    a scepter of justice will be the scepter of your kingdom.

You love righteousness and hate wickedness;

    therefore God, your God, has set you

        above your companions

    by anointing you with the oil of joy.

All your robes are fragrant with myrrh and aloes and cassia;

    from palaces adorned with ivory

    the music of the strings makes you glad.

Daughters of kings are among your honored women;

    at your right hand is the royal bride in gold of Ophir.

Listen, daughter, and pay careful attention:

    Forget your people and your father's house.

Let the king be enthralled by your beauty;

honor him, for he is your lord.
The city of Tyre will come with a gift,
people of wealth will seek your favor.
All glorious is the princess within her chamber;
her gown is interwoven with gold.
In embroidered garments she is led to the king;
her virgin companions follow her—
those brought to be with her.
Led in with joy and gladness,
they enter the palace of the king.
Your sons will take the place of your fathers;
you will make them princes throughout the land.
I will perpetuate your memory through all generations;
therefore, the nations will praise you
for ever and ever." (Psalm 45:1-17)

If there is one charge that can be levelled at Christianity and Judaism together, it's that the Bible gets chopped up to fit one's own preconceived ideas. We accept *this*, but we don't accept *so on and so forth* (Luke 24:26-27). The Jews want an earthly kingdom and Christians want a heavenly one. It all boils down, I believe, to God's people largely accepting only the good things that the Bible must say while neglecting, and even rejecting, the hard and difficult things.

Certainly, one need only look at the topic of climate change to see how guilty each party is for being ignorant of what the scriptures teach on this important and vital topic. The study of climate change reveals to us the truth of God's work, and how it follows Chiliasm. As for an earthly and heavenly kingdom, both are clearly taught in the scriptures. The New Testament complements the Old Testament and vice versa. What Christianity and Judaism should have done is simply *believe* what the scriptures say, period! They should have all paid attention to this:

> *He said to them, "How foolish you are, and how slow to believe all that the prophets have spoken! Did not the Messiah have to suffer these things and then enter his glory?" And beginning with Moses and all the Prophets, he explained to them what was said in all the Scriptures concerning himself."*
> *(Luke 24:25-27)*

Who then is the elect of God? Those who have faith in Christ Jesus, both Jew and Gentile. St. Paul referred to it this way:

> *"No, a person is a Jew who is one inwardly; and circumcision is circumcision of the heart, by the Spirit, not by the written code. Such a person's praise is not from other people, but from God." (Romans 2:29)*

In the Kingdom age, this will play itself out. At that time, no Jew will do what they do now, which is to hate and even curse the Messiah; instead they will know Him, and intimately so. It's why we read in Zechariah:

> *"This is what the Lord Almighty says: "In those days ten people from all languages and nations will take firm hold of one Jew by the hem of his robe and say, 'Let us go with you, because we have heard that God is with you." (Zechariah 8:23)*

This is, of course, about the Feast of Tabernacles, a glorious birthday party for the ages!

Epilogue

Having considered the truth concerning Gog and Magog and the Feast of Tabernacles, it would be beneficial to look more intently at the book of Zechariah and ask ourselves how knowing the above applies to the other prophecies there? Especially intriguing is whether the prophecy of Gog and Magog exists within this book (Zechariah 12). It's an important question because if Gog and Magog are referenced by Zechariah, it sheds an enormous amount of light on the major events of the prophetic calendar.

I will examine this by working backwards, from the end to the beginning.

Zechariah 14:16–21 is a restatement of Zechariah 13:1–6, covering the arrival of the millennial kingdom under Christ Jesus. The all-important issue here is the Feast of Tabernacles and its connection to rain. It goes back to that promise of rain from Deuteronomy 11:17, except this time the rain will cover the entire planet. Imagine: if someone doesn't go to Jerusalem for the Feast of Tabernacles during the millennial period, they will receive no rain from God. Amazing!

Zechariah 14:12–15 speaks to the coming Armageddon. It is comparable to what we see in Revelation 16:17–21.

Zechariah 14:10 covers the start of the millennial kingdom wherein Christ Jesus will reign for a thousand years.

Zechariah 14:1–9 restates what is written in Zechariah 12:10–14, completely agreeing with what is found in Revelation 16:12–16.

Zechariah 13:8–9 talks about what happened to Israel at our Lord's crucifixion and in the decades, that followed. It speaks of the Roman occupation and how two-thirds were literally struck down but a third of the people were saved because they believed and were by their sufferings purified, including the very apostles of Christ. This passage has nothing to do with today, or the future for that matter. It's also significant that the same is written about in Daniel 12:10. It raises the theological issue that there very well could be a great deal of truth to the idea that God isn't finished with any of us.

Zechariah 13:7 talks about the suffering of our Lord Christ Jesus.

Zechariah 13:1–6 marks the beginning of the millennial kingdom upon the earth. This entire chapter deals with the remorse and guilt of those Jews who survive Armageddon to see Christ Jesus and the pain of realizing the errors of their ways. This realization leads them to total obedience, even under penalty of death by their own family members. What's left of Israel will finally come to their senses!

Zechariah 12:10–14 speaks of the coming of Christ, which is agrees completely with Revelation 16:12–16.

Zechariah 12:1–9 speaks of the battle of Gog and Magog. I am sure of this because of verses 3 and 9, which are comparable to Revelation 20. Beyond that, the people of Jerusalem are God's and God is theirs. This is speaking about the millennial kingdom and an Israel that includes all believers, which is what is taught in Romans 11:17 (the hybrid plant and the first resurrection)!

Zechariah 11:12–13 speaks of our Lord Christ Jesus and the price paid for Him, thirty pieces of silver. As for the rest of the chapter, it would certainly have to be the history of Roman rule. God speaks of breaking His covenant and Zechariah 11:6 provides an excellent illustration of the history of that period. Unlike previous generations, God did nothing to rescue the Jewish nation from their oppressors under Roman rule. God simply left it all to Caesar!

Zechariah 10 seems to talk about the time of the restoration of all things, comparable to Zechariah 13–14 and the arrival of the millennial kingdom. Verse 4 contains another reference to our Lord and Saviour Christ Jesus. Beyond that, it's interesting that the chapter begins with the weather—rain. This is surely no coincidence, given the promise of rain back in Deuteronomy 11:17 and how it fits with the Feast of Tabernacles. This makes me think that Zechariah 10 has more to do with the arrival of the millennial kingdom than anything having to do with 1948, which increasingly appears to be a self-fulfilling prophecy by those who wished to push up God's timetable. In fact, I would venture to say that 1948 has more to do with what Christ spoke about in John 10:1: *"Very truly I tell you Pharisees, anyone who does not enter the sheep pen by the gate, but climbs in by some other way, is a thief and a robber."* He addressed this to the Pharisees, peculiarly enough. There isn't a rabbi in the last one hundred years, if not the last two thousand, that cares to go through the door that is Christ. It's interesting that Christ in John 1:2-3 speaks about the deceit and lies and lack of a real shepherd. Wow! That perfectly explains the history of the last hundred years.

Zechariah 9 again speaks about the coming of the Messiah (Zechariah 9:9-10) and then goes on to speak about His governmental rule and the Lord finally appearing. This surely must be Armageddon, comparable to Revelation 16:17-21 and the restoration of all things during the millennial period.

Zechariah 8 addresses the millennial kingdom, and we can know this by the one verse which proves it perfectly (Zechariah 8:3). Christ will come to Jerusalem and make His home there.

Zechariah 7 is nothing more than the history of the current period. Perhaps Zechariah 7:13-14 fulfil the final diaspora of the Jews to the four corners of the earth during the Roman expulsions. The Bar Kochba revolt sums up perfectly the words of our Lord in verse 13, if not Christ's own words in the gospels.

Zechariah 6 speaks of our Lord as the Branch. Beyond that, it seems to be a mixture of current events culminating with what will happen under the rulership of Christ after He returns.

Zechariah 5 is interesting in that it speaks of a woman in a basket who is taken to the country of Babylonia. The most significant matter here is how she is described as "wickedness." In Revelation 17:5, we have the prophecy of *"a mystery, 'BABYLON THE GREAT, THE MOTHER OF PROSTITUTES, AND OF THE ABOMINATIONS OF THE EARTH.'"*

Zechariah 4 contains the story of two olive trees, apparently signifying two men. The significant issue here is our further knowledge of them in Revelation 11:5–11, where we find them witnessing and evangelizing for the Lord in Jerusalem—using the weather, no less.

Zechariah 3 seems to provide a mixture of current events culminating with the prophecy of Christ as the Branch, as well as His return to Jerusalem which will bring an end to all sin in a single day. This again is comparable to Armageddon, written about in Zechariah 14:10.

Zechariah 2 speaks of the millennial period. Perhaps the most significant matter is that the people will escape from Babylon, which is comparable to what is written in Revelation 18:4: *"Then I heard another voice from heaven say: 'Come out of her, my people,' so that you will not share in her sins, so that you will not receive any of her plagues."*

Zechariah 1, starting with the horns in verse 18, signify kings and nations. The Lord is no doubt talking about the same nations we hear about in the book of Daniel—Rome, Greece, Media-Persia, and Babylon. The rest of the chapter appears to be a synopsis of Israel's history, with a view to what her future will finally look like under Christ Jesus the Nazarene.

www.ingramcontent.com/pod-product-compliance
Lightning Source LLC
Chambersburg PA
CBHW030916080526
44589CB00010B/325